JUNIOR SEAU

Overcoming the Odds

D1248743

by

Jim Trotter

SPORTS PUBLISHING INC.
www.SportsPublishingInc.com

Production manager: Susan M. McKinney
Production coordinator: Erin J. Sands
Series editor: Rob Rains
Cover design: Scot Muncaster/Todd Lauer
Photo coordinator: Claudia Mitroi
Photos: AP/Wide World Photos, Brian Spurlock and Joe Robbins, Oceanside
High School

ISBN: 1-58261-169-6
Library of Congress Catalog Card Number: 99-68302

SPORTS PUBLISHING INC.
SportsPublishingInc.com

Printed in the United States.

Contents

Junior has been selected for eight consecutive Pro Bowls.
(Brian Spurlock)

The 1998 Season

Before the start of each football season, the San Diego Chargers hold a kickoff luncheon for sponsors and dignitaries. Last August was no exception. The Chargers showed a highlight film, had their coaches and officials say a few words and then handed out team awards from the previous season.

Pro Bowl linebacker Junior Seau is usually a rock in such situations. He rises from his seat, gives thanks to those around him and says how excited he is about the coming season. He even tosses in a

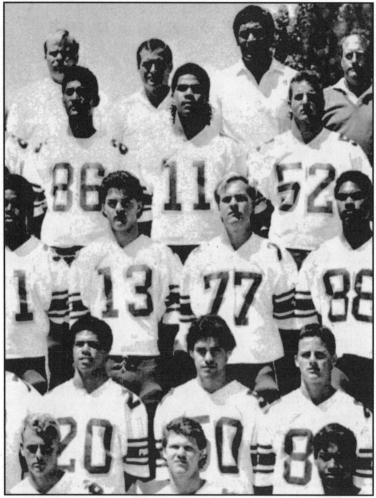

Junior (11) played high school football at Oceanside High School. (Oceanside High School)

few one-liners to brighten an already beaming room.

But things were different at the 1998 luncheon. Junior, the Gibraltar of San Diego's defense, was showing signs of cracking. His voice quivered and his eyes welled. He was wearing slacks and a polo shirt, but his soul was naked.

The previous 12 months had been a trying time for him. It began with him tearing knee cartilage in a preseason game in 1997. The injury forced him to miss the season opener and reminded him that the end of his career could be a play away.

Then there were the ups and downs associated with negotiating a contract extension. As much as he tried to stay even-keeled, the talks weighed on his mind. The longer they went, the more he felt the club was not recognizing his contributions on the field and in the community.

The sides finally agreed to terms on a $27.1 million extension in September, but instead of things getting better, they continued to spiral downward.

The Chargers suffered through a 4-12 season, their first losing record since 1992, and six months later Junior was criticized for not attending the opening of a voluntary mini-camp. Management accused him of being selfish and hinted that he was unhappy with his contract. Fans reacted with anger and disappointment.

Junior cut short his family vacation to return to the camp, but the unkind words didn't end there. They continued in training camp and picked up steam after Junior blocked prized rookie quarterback Ryan Leaf to the ground after Leaf threw an interception in practice.

The move was a rite of passage for the rookie, but reporters and fans tried to turn it into more than that. There was talk that Junior's ego was bruised by all the attention Leaf was receiving, not to mention the $11.25 million signing bonus the team awarded the former Washington State star.

Privately, Junior wondered what went wrong. How could fans in the area where he had grown up, the people who had followed him during his standout careers at Oceanside High School and the University of Southern California, doubt what he was all about?

Winning is the only thing that matters to him on the football field. If having players such as Leaf on the roster would help accomplish that, he is all for that. Somewhere along the way that got lost amid the headlines and speculation. Suddenly Junior was portrayed as the bad guy, and it hurt.

As he stood at the kickoff luncheon to accept the team MVP award for 1997, an emotional Junior took the microphone and tried to locate his wife, Gina. He thanked her for being his rock through the hard times. He told her how he could not have gotten through it without her. Then he went out and did the only thing he knows how to do: fight to overcome adversity.

He did it as a child, rising above the economic and social barriers that blocked his way after moving from American Samoa to Oceanside at the age of seven. He did it at Southern Cal, where some people viewed him as a "dumb jock" after he was ruled ineligible as a freshman because he failed to achieve the necessary qualifying score on a college entrance exam.

He did it again in 1998, quietly earning his eighth consecutive trip to the Pro Bowl. He took passion and preparation and molded it into arguably his finest season as a pro. His 115 tackles led the team, and his 3.5 sacks ranked near the top.

Some of the success had to do with better study habits. Junior spent more time watching videotapes, looking for opponents' tendencies and trying to figure out how they might attack him so he could turn around and use it against them. In previous seasons, he would take tapes home and toss them on the couch so he could play with his kids in the pool.

Junior had matured as a player. He understood that he could no longer rely solely on his athleticism. Father Time eventually takes a step away from everyone, and Junior was not going to wait until the last moment to prepare himself for that. So he studied like he never had before.

There were changes in Junior off the field, too. People around the training complex talked of how he was more relaxed, more at ease last season.

"Whenever you have peace within yourself, it spreads out," Junior said during the season. "It's a light. I have peace in my heart. My faith is a lot stronger."

***The 1997 season was a difficult one for Junior.
(Joe Robbins)***

That is not to say the fallout from all the things that went on in the off-season and at the start of training camp didn't hurt him deeply. They did, though people beyond his immediate circle of family and friends had no idea how much.

"It hurt a lot," said Junior's wife, Gina. "It was humbling for him to read that and for us to receive hate mail. There are a lot of little bits of things that we've gone through the last several years, and we've learned a lot from them. When you're high, everyone's on you. And when you're low, it felt like people were kicking the dog when it's down for no reason.

"I think this year Junior's just a lot more balanced in everything. He's maturing leaps and bounds, spiritually and as a man. He's getting his priorities straight and really eliminating a lot of these so-called friends and acquaintances that seem to pop up everywhere in people's lives, especially athletes who have a little bit of fame."

Junior said the experiences taught him that the game is bigger than any one individual, no matter how talented or popular. It also reminded him that some people will try to tear you down as quickly as they built you up.

"It just shows that you can do a lot of things and no matter where you sit statistically and in the eyes of man, there's always the opportunity to be judged wrong," said Junior. "For me to see that is humbling. It helped me as a person, and it built all of us—me and my family."

That's the reason Junior wanted to acknowledge his wife at the kickoff luncheon. Football and fans won't always be there, but family will be. And Gina's love and support were more important to him than any game or award.

"He knows family is all he's got," said Gina. "They're going to stand by him through thick and thin, through good and bad. When this is all over, when this NFL ride is said and done, we're going to be the ones standing right next to him."

*Junior was voted "Most Athletic" at Oceanside High School.
(Oceanside High School)*

CHAPTER TWO

The Early Years

Oceanside is a coastal city about 30 miles north of San Diego. Look west and you will see a gentle surf rolling over a sandy shore. You'll also see sunsets worthy of postcards.

But look east and the area's natural beauty gives way to poverty; to communities where gangs and violence are a part of everyday life.

This is where Junior grew up.

He lived in a two-bedroom house with his mother and father and five brothers and sisters. The place was so small that Junior and his two brothers used the garage as their bedroom. When the girls joked that their bedroom had carpeting, the boys countered that they had the biggest door in the house.

The garage wasn't always comfortable. The boys slept on mattresses on the ground and used portable heaters in the winter. It was so cold some nights they could see their breath when they exhaled.

Junior looks back on those times with a smile. He wouldn't change them for anything. You had to have been there to understand why.

"I think everyone in the National Football League has a sob story to tell," said Junior. "I'm not the only one in the league who lived that way. But I'll tell you this much, what I went through helped me get to where I am today."

His boyhood days, his struggles, helped mold him into the person he is. They taught him to appreciate what he has—the beautiful home in La Jolla, the refrigerator full of food, the closets full of clothes, the security of not having to wonder how he's going to pay for his kids' college education.

Junior has never forgotten where he came from. In fact, he is as much a part of the community today as he was as a youngster. He established a teen center at the Boys & Girls Club of Oceanside and helped stock it with weight-training equipment and computers. The kids were so appreciative, they named it Club 55 after Junior, whose jersey number is 55.

Junior also is a regular in the community. He attends high school games, talks to kids at assemblies and visits with those less fortunate. He can't do everything for everyone, but he wants to

Junior (far right) poses with his high school teammates.
(Oceanside High School)

be a role model for kids looking to improve themselves.

Tiaina and Luisa, Junior's parents, tried to help their children avoid the drugs and gangs in the neighborhood by keeping them busy with school and sports and other activities. Religion was also important in their house.

Tiaina, after whom Junior is named, was a deacon in the First Samoan Congregational Church, and every Sunday he would drive the family to Sunday services. He also led prayers twice a day at home.

During the week, Tiaina Sr. worked as a custodian at a local high school. Solidly built, he presented an intimidating figure, particularly when his children strayed from the acceptable path. A wrong step, one brother once said, could result in spankings with sticks, shoes or whatever happened to be lying around.

"Dad taught us about morals, values and goals," said Junior. "Having a tight-knit family was important to him."

Tiaina and Luisa were born in American Samoa, a U.S. territory located in the South Pacific. It is comprised of seven tropical islands about 1,600 miles northeast of New Zealand. Tiaina and Luisa, who lived on the island of Aunuu, moved their family to San Diego in 1964 and spent five years there before returning to American Samoa shortly after Junior was born on January 19, 1969.

They eventually chose to return to San Diego for good, and the family settled in Oceanside. They brought relatively little money and clothing with them, but they did have their religion and customs, and they instilled them in their kids.

The Seaus spoke only Samoan and dressed in traditional island clothing while at home. The sisters would don muumuus, long, colorful, loose-fitting, dresses; and the brothers would wear lavalavas, wrap-around skirts. The kids also practiced traditional dances. For the boys, that meant the Samoan slap dance. For the girls, it meant the hula.

Junior spoke only Samoan when he returned to the continental U.S. shortly before kindergarten, and consequently he struggled in school. He kept working at it, and by the time he finished elementary school, he was speaking both Samoan and English.

It was about this time that his love of athletics was developing. His older brothers were competing in different sports, and Junior wanted to be just like them. Actually, he wanted to be better than them, especially when he was the last person unclaimed when teams chose up sides.

Junior (#40) proved up to the challenge of playing defense in basketball as well. (Oceanside High School)

Junior was unusually well coordinated for his age. He also was tall, fast and strong. What set him apart from other kids his age, however, was his competitiveness. No matter what the sport, he wanted to win. He had to win.

He wanted to compete in organized sports, but his parents rarely had the money for the registration fees. So, Junior spent much of his time at the local Boys & Girls club, where his teams almost always won.

His reputation was growing faster than his body at this time. His school, Jefferson Junior High, became a magnet for local high school coaches who wanted him to attend their schools. Some people thought he would attend El Camino, where his father was a custodian. But Junior chose to stay and attend Oceanside High.

Junior (11) decided to attend Oceanside High School instead of transferring to El Camino or Vista High. (Oceanside High School)

High School

Junior's decision to enroll at Oceanside High as a freshman in 1983 shocked some people in the community. They wondered why an athlete of his ability would go to a school whose football team had not had a winning season in six years instead of a nearby school with a strong program.

He could have gotten an intra-district transfer to attend El Camino High, the city's more modern and more successful school, because his father was a custodian there. Or he could have capitalized on a quirk in school-boundary lines and attended Vista High, which, at the time, had one of the state's top football programs.

But the decision was a no-brainer for Junior. His two older brothers were Pirates at Oceanside High, and he was going to be a Pirate, not a Wildcat or a Longhorn.

"Family and loyalty are everything in life," Junior said. "I could have left Oceanside High; I had every opportunity. But I figured, 'Why go to a winner and be just another guy?' I wanted to stay and help my school become a winner. It was a tough choice, but leaving would have been against everything I believe in."

It didn't take long for Junior to open eyes at his new school. As a 6-foot, 200-pound freshman, he earned a starting spot as a defensive end on the junior varsity football team. He also was the backup quarterback.

To him, there was nothing better than being on the field in the heat of the battle. It was the food that filled him, the balm that soothed him, the vehicle that carried him away from his problems.

His parents knew his talents were special, and they did what they could to help him succeed. Instead of requiring him to work after school to help ease the family's financial burdens, as they had done with the older kids, Tiaina and his wife excused Junior so he could concentrate on athletics.

It was an extraordinary privilege for someone so young.

"The opportunity was special in my family," said Junior. "It's not a debt or something I feel I have to pay back. It's something you respect."

Junior's family was always there to cheer him on. (Brian Spurlock)

Junior never had to look up in the stands to know his family was behind him. At any given time, his mom, dad, brothers, sisters, aunts, uncles and cousins were there cheering him on and providing him with motivation.

One of Junior's former coaches said family members would even chip in and reward Junior for outstanding plays. A sack might bring him $10. Ditto an interception.

"One day they paid up and he had a wad of bills that could choke a horse," Bill Christopher, one of his high school coaches, told *The New York Times*.

As much as Junior loved playing for his family, the internal pressure could be great. He would become tight, overly intense. His coaches tried to remind him to loosen up and enjoy the games for what they are—games—but it was hard for Junior.

Everyone looked up to him, and, at times, it weighed on him. Teammates marveled at his athletic ability, work habits and never-say-die attitude; and family members puffed out their chests a little farther each time he made a big play.

If there was one person Junior wanted to please more than anyone else, it was his father. Tiaina was demanding and imposing. Junior's friends used to stand in the middle of the street and call for him to come out and play because they were afraid of knocking on the door and having Tiaina answer.

Junior and his brothers were just as fearful on occasions. Such times usually came after they lost a game. Tiaina often responded to defeats in two ways; he would ignore the boys altogether or criticize them for not working hard enough.

"If we lost, Dad would act like we were failures," Junior's brother Savaii once said. "He'd say, 'You're lazy.'"

Even as a youngster, Junior was never lazy. It was not uncommon for him to lift weights before his brothers awoke in the morning or be out of the house before his siblings got out of bed. A school employee once stumbled upon Junior doing push-ups and sit-ups and shuttle runs outside the school weight room at 7:30 in the morning in the summer.

The evenings brought similar workouts—hundreds of push-ups and sit-ups and dozens of chin-ups from the limb of a tree in the backyard. The harder he pushed himself, the more he liked it.

Frustratingly for Junior, the hard work did not translate into winning seasons when he joined the varsity as a sophomore. The Pirates finished 5-5 his first season and 3-7 his junior season. That

In 1986, Charger quarterback Dan Fouts (right) presented Junior with the Parade Magazine *All-American Football Athlete Award. (Oceanside High School)*

made it eight consecutive non-winning seasons entering his senior year, and Junior was determined to end the streak there.

He came through in a big way as the Pirates finished 10-3 and advanced to the CIF-San Diego Section finals for the first time since 1975. They lost to powerful Lincoln Prep in the championship game, 41-7, but to their classmates they were athletic heroes.

The football season was the start of a memorable senior year for Junior. He started at linebacker and wide receiver/tight end, and made his presence felt on both sides of the ball. He had 123 tackles, 14 sacks and five interceptions on defense, and 71 receptions for 1,115 yards and 15 touchdowns on offense. He was voted the San Diego County Defensive Player of the Year, and the Avocado League Offensive Player of the Year. He also was named to

Junior receives his high school basketball award.
(Oceanside High School)

Parade Magazine's All-America team.

Then he was named the county's basketball Player of the Year after leading Oceanside to the Avocado League title. He also had the league's best shotput that spring. But football was his sport.

Recruiting letters were coming from everywhere, and when Junior selected the University of Southern California, many assumed he would be another in a long line of great linebackers to play at USC. Little did he realize that a blindside hit was waiting for him.

Junior participated in football, basketball and track and field at Oceanside.
(Oceanside High School)

Blindsided

Junior wasn't serious about his studies his first year at Oceanside High, and it showed on his report card. He had other things on his mind, like football, basketball, track and field and baseball.

But that changed the following year, when Junior earned straight A's as a sophomore. And again as a junior. And also as a senior to graduate with a 3.6 grade-point average.

Even so, Junior did not score high enough on a college entrance exam to be eligible for freshman football at USC. He became a casualty of relatively new NCAA legislation known as Proposition 48, which required incoming freshman to score a minimum of 700 on the Scholastic Aptitude Test in order to be eligible for intercollegiate athletics.

Junior did well on the math portion but struggled on the verbal part. His combined score of 690 left him 10 points shy of achieving the mandatory qualifying score.

The news hurt Junior more than any hit he had sustained on the football field. He felt he had brought shame on his family's proud name. He also was concerned that people would look down on his high school.

"Everything I worked for, everything my family had stood for was gone," he said. "I was labeled a dumb jock."

Junior felt helpless and alone. That fall, during an assembly at Oceanside High School, he apologized to the students and faculty for letting them down. The words came from the heart. So did the emotion that coated them.

Junior returned to the school that spring and spoke to the kids again, stressing the importance of education. If he could help just one kid not go through the same thing he was experiencing, then his setback would not be in vain.

But that is not to say life without football was easy. Junior went from being a three-sport guy in high school to being a no-sport guy in college. He could not practice with the team, and couldn't watch film with the other players. He felt ostracized. It was as if he had been branded a "Prop 48 Dummy."

"I went from prep star to the biggest failure in the world," said Junior. "That year was the true

The Chargers superstar played college football for USC.
(Brian Spurlock)

test of believing in myself. I tasted life early. But I grew up as a man and a student."

Junior returned to the field as a sophomore, but no one treated him like a Parade All-American. He was third on the depth chart. It didn't help that in his first practice, during a pass-rush drill, he took a swipe at the ball and caught a finger in another player's helmet.

His finger was severely cut. Doctors closed the wound and placed his hand in a cast. While that stabilized the finger, it did little to numb the pain Junior experienced each time his hand took a hit. The finger was so sensitive it sent currents of pain up his arm whenever he moved his hand.

He returned to practice after sitting out for two days, but soon badly sprained an ankle. The injuries limited his playing time and prevented him from showing what he could really do. He wound up playing on special teams and as a backup linebacker.

At the end of the season, the team held an awards banquet. Junior, the former all-everything, didn't even receive a certificate. It was a humbling moment for someone with his athletic pedigree.

"That's when I dedicated myself to becoming an All-American," he would say later.

Going into his third season, Trojans head coach Larry Smith named Junior the starter at outside linebacker. It didn't take long for the Oceanside native to make an impact.

In the second game, he had three sacks in a 66-10 victory over Utah State. The next week, in a 42-3 drubbing of Ohio State, he had two sacks, four QB pressures and four pass deflections. People were beginning to take notice.

Later, Junior had three sacks against Stanford and four against Oregon State. His season was interrupted in the regular-season finale against UCLA, when Junior sustained a separated shoulder. But he returned in time to play in the Rose Bowl game against Michigan State.

Junior, all but invisible his first two years in Los Angeles, finished the season with a team-record 19 sacks. He also was voted the Trojans' MVP and was named to a handful of All-America teams. The Pacific 10 Conference also named him its Defensive Player of the Year.

All the questions had been answered except for one: Would Junior return for his senior season?

Junior skipped his final year of college to enter the NFL draft.
(Joe Robbins)

CHAPTER FIVE

Making the Jump

It used to be that players spent four years in college before entering the NFL draft. But the seeds of change were planted in the early '80s, when running back Herschel Walker left the University of Georgia after his junior season to play in the United States Football League.

Some people assumed the move would flood the National Football League with players leaving college early. But it wasn't until 1989 that the first wave began. Oklahoma State running Barry Sanders started it by declaring for the draft after winning the Heisman Trophy as a junior. When the Detroit Lions selected him with the third pick, college players in Los Angeles and Miami and all points in between sat up and took notice.

Junior was entering his junior season at USC at the time, and in the back of his mind he knew the riches were there for him if he could put together a stellar season. It had been his dream since he was in grade school to be a member of the NFL's exclusive fraternity, and when he went out and had a record-setting season in his third year at USC, the dream was staring in his face.

But instead of him jumping at it, Junior waffled. He wanted the financial security an NFL contract could provide him and his family, but he also wanted to get his degree. Education was important to his parents, and getting his degree in public administration would be the ultimate comeback for people who viewed him as a "Prop 48 Dummy."

Junior talked to family and friends about what he should do. USC coach Larry Smith advised him to make the jump only if he was going to be a first-round pick. Since there was little question about that, Junior, with the blessing of his parents, declared himself eligible for the draft.

The San Diego Chargers, *his* San Diego Chargers, selected him with the fifth pick of the entire draft. The occasion moved him beyond words. He not only had financial security but also the rare good fortune of being selected by his hometown team. The smile on his face seemed permanent.

Unfortunately for Junior, the rest of the year was not as memorable. Things got off on the wrong foot when he and the Chargers could not agree on contract terms before the start of training camp.

The Chargers chose Junior with the fifth pick in the NFL draft. (Joe Robbins)

Even when Junior accepted a four-year, $4.5 million deal, he admitted that he nearly backed out of the agreement.

He took the field for the first time in the preseason finale against the Raiders in Los Angeles. It was understood that he would not start the game, but no one realized he wouldn't finish it. He was ejected after two plays for throwing a punch at an offensive lineman.

Things got worse from there. He contributed to a Dallas Cowboys scoring drive by receiving a 15-yard penalty for spearing. He also aided the Houston Oilers' game-winning possession with a 15-yard penalty for unsportsmanlike conduct. He was cited for "leaping" while trying to block a field-goal attempt.

What hurt Junior most, however, was hearing San Diegans boo him during pregame introductions at the Chargers' home opener. He tried to act as if he didn't hear them, but the warrior was wounded. He had grown up with these fans, his fans, and now they had turned on him.

At times, Junior appeared overwhelmed. He was trying to do so much that he was doing very little. The more he struggled, the more he pressed. And the more he pressed, the more he struggled.

It didn't help that the Chargers had him playing inside linebacker when all of his success at USC was on the outside. With the Trojans, he was responsible only for rushing the quarterback in passing situations. He did not have to know pass coverages or defensive schemes. He simply had to pin back his ears and go.

Junior hated the switch. And he hated being pulled from the game on third down because pass coverage was new to him. Training camp would have helped, but he missed all but one week because of his contract impasse.

"I haven't gone out there on the field yet feeling like Junior Seau the football player," Junior said at the time. "I had high expectations—and I still do. But there are things I've just got to learn.

"Right now, it's more than a chore to come to work because I put a lot of pressure on myself. I gotta do something."

Junior was fighting an internal battle. The more he struggled, the more he wanted to take his talents and move outside, where he was comfortable. But Junior had to come to the realization that he couldn't succeed by fighting himself. He had to accept his role, no matter how much he didn't like it.

Defensive coordinator Ron Lynn tried to sell him on the change by appealing to his ego. He would tell Junior there could be glory on the inside, too. He preached that Junior could be one of the greatest inside linebackers to ever play the game.

The more Lynn talked, the more Junior listened.

Grudgingly.

"I think Junior can be the dominant guy in the league at his position," Lynn once told the *Los Angeles Times*. "I don't see anyone else on the horizon. Name another inside linebacker. Shane Conlan? Shane Conlan can't carry this guy's helmet."

Gradually, Junior began improving. Despite being on the sideline on third downs, he still finished second on the team with 85 tackles. And despite managing just one tackle, which came in the season finale, he still was named an alternate on the American Football Conference Pro Bowl squad.

Through all the struggles, through all the internal battles, through all the 10 losses in 16 games, Junior showed enough to earn the respect of opponents and fans, not to mention his teammates. A star was born, and Junior was not about to stop there.

In 1991, his second season, he led the team with 129 tackles, was second in sacks with seven, and was an all-AFC choice at middle linebacker. The next year, he again led the club in tackles despite missing a game, was the only unanimous choice on the all-AFC team, was named the Defensive Player of the Year by Football Digest, and helped the Chargers reach the playoffs for the first time since 1982.

They beat the Kansas City Chiefs, 17-0, in the first round of the playoffs, but lost to the Miami Dolphins, 31-0, the following week. Junior, who had been a regular in the postseason at USC, where the Trojans went to three straight Rose Bowls during his time there, was so happy about getting to the postseason with San Diego that he thanked the fans by spending $14,000 on a full-page adver-

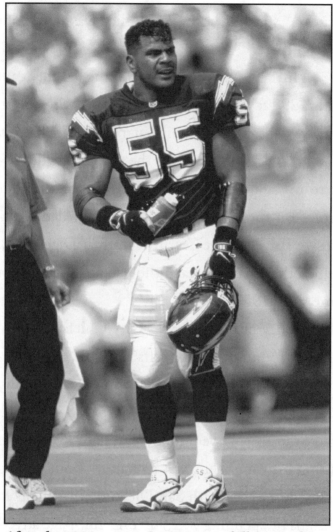

***After the 1991 season, Junior put a full-page ad in
the* San Diego Union-Tribune *thanking the fans for
a wonderful year. (Joe Robbins)***

tisement in the *San Diego Union-Tribune*.

The ad featured photos of Chargers fans and the words: "TO THE FANS OF SAN DIEGO, I THANK YOU FOR A WONDERFUL YEAR. JUNIOR SEAU AND FAMILY."

Junior always tries to be thoughtful towards his fans.
(AP/Wide World Photos)

CHAPTER SIX

Giving Back

Junior never wants to close the door on his past and forget where he comes from, so every year he gathers some of his football friends for a charity golf event in a San Diego suburb. The list of past and present stars who agree to attend always reads like a who's who of NFL greats: Jerry Rice, Ronnie Lott, Lance Alworth, Bruce Smith, Deacon Jones, and Marcus Allen.

Yet some of the biggest names associated with

the event belong to people you've never heard of. One of them is Augrista Belford.

It was in 1994 that the Junior Seau Foundation began doing what it could to help send needy high schoolers to college, and Belford, an Oceanside native, was among the first group of students to receive assistance.

When she walked across the stage at Cal State Northridge in 1999 to receive her bachelor's in pyschology, it brought a smile to only her face, but also that of Junior.

"There are a lot of great things that have happened to me throughout my career, but nothing can ever replace the thrill I get from making a significant impact in someone's life," said Junior. "What we wanted to do with the foundation was use it as a vehicle to reach out to the youth of San Diego.

"And while we can't control every aspect of the youth in San Diego, we can do our part. Then hopefully after everything is said and done, we can say we accomplished our goal."

The Junior Seau Foundation was established in 1992 by Junior and his wife, Gina. Their goal was to raise money and resources for programs that would help at-risk kids in San Diego County overcome the obstacles they face each day.

The couple initially ran the business out of their home, but after two years they were forced to set up permanent lodging elsewhere because the foundation was growing so quickly. In 1999, it was contributing $250,000 to $400,000 annually to various causes, particularly in the inner city.

Junior also contributes his time and resources in other ways. He donated the weight-training equipment to the Oceanside Boys & Girls Club

Junior became a member of The Boys & Girls Club of America's National Alumni Hall of Fame in 1999. (Joe Robbins)

and helped secure computers for the teen center. His work with the facility resulted in The Boys & Girls Club of America inducting him into its National Alumni Hall of Fame in the spring of 1999.

He also takes time to speak to servicemen stationed in San Diego County. His appearance on one naval ship was so special they used it as the lead story on the military national news, beaming it U.S. military facilities and naval ships around the world.

But Junior's heart is with the children. That's the primary reason the foundation was established.

"There's nothing that I wouldn't do for the Junior Seau Foundation," said Belford. "The appreciation that I have for him goes beyond words. I used to watch him when he was in high school and I never knew he would have this kind of impact on my life. It's been tremendous."

The Jets' Keyshawn Johnson and Junior walk off the field with smiles on their faces during a Pro Bowl game. (AP/Wide World Photos)

7

Reality Check

Junior should have been riding high in 1993. His position among his peers was unquestioned, his team was coming off its first playoff appearance in 10 years and his wife was pregnant with their first child.

Life was good. Real good. Maybe too good.

The Seaus received a reality check in August when Gina gave birth six weeks premature to daughter Sydney Beau. The baby's lungs weren't fully developed and there was concern she might not live. The news nearly floored Junior, who learned shortly after that his 16-year-old brother, Tony, had been charged with attempted murder in a gang-related incident.

One crisis was bad enough. Two seemed unfair.

Junior searched for meaning where there was none. He was accustomed to handling things, to having a hand in determining the outcome of a situation. But now he was helpless. All he could do was pray.

He thought about leaving the team for a while, but his family told him to do his job. Junior tried to go on, and to the naked eye, he was his same old self in helping the Chargers finish 8-8. He led the team with 129 tackles, tying his career high, and earned a third straight spot on the All-Pro team.

But those close to Junior knew he was struggling, on the field and off. His mind just wasn't there.

"What he had to deal with was an unusual set of circumstances and I don't think you can fault him," said coach Bobby Ross. "Any of us as people would have a difficult time dealing with that. I think he was able to function well considering everything. Don't forget, he had a Pro Bowl year and that wasn't a cheap Pro Bowl year and on a team that didn't do quite as well as it did the previous year. It was a stressful year for him, and I think he handled it well."

"It definitely was the toughest year that I had to go through," said Junior. "Normally, your opponents, you can study. And you can work out and study and come out all right.

"But when it pertains to life, you're in the Lord's hands and patience has to kick in. Things

Junior is an emotional player on the field.
(AP/Wide World Photos)

are out of your control, and that year was out of my control. I had never experienced wanting something so bad, and yet there was nothing you could do. You would look at your wife and she would be crying and there was nothing you could do about it. Whenever you have a loved one, and you feel the love for them, and you can't bring a smile to their face, it hurts."

Smiles returned to the Seau's family as the year went on. Sydney pulled through just fine, with proud papa joking at one point that she was growing so fast she was slightly overweight. And Tony was sentenced to 10 years in a California Youth Authority facility after pleading guilty.

His sentence brought a sigh of relief from the family. After all, things could have been worse. A lot worse. Tony could have killed someone—or been killed himself.

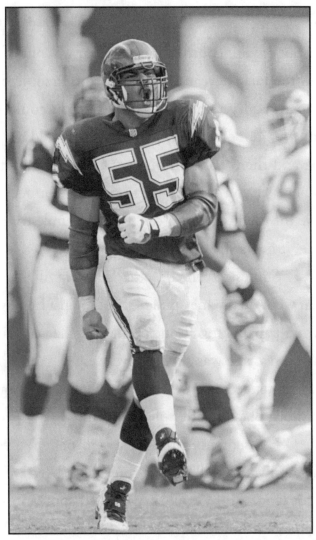

Despite some hard times, things are looking good for Junior. (AP/Wide World Photos)

Bouncing Back Strong

If 1993 was the worst year of Junior's fooball life, 1994 was the best. He had a healthy daughter and wife, a new four-year, $16 million contract that made him one of the NFL's highest-paid defensive players and high hopes that good things were ahead for the Chargers. His optimism was borne out in the season opener, when the Chargers held off the Denver Broncos on the road.

Junior comes up with a key interception.
(AP/Wide World Photos)

The Broncos appeared to have the Chargers just where they wanted them. They had the ball within the shadows of the goal line. They had John Elway, the master of the fourth-quarter comeback, at quarterback. And they had a raucous crowd at their back.

When Elway dropped back to pass and rolled to the right, the crowd and the expectations rose. Then it happened, a sign that the Chargers were destined for a special year. Elway cocked his right arm, pulled the trigger and ... lost the ball.

Junior smothered the ball just before stepping out of bounds, setting off a wild celebration along the San Diego sideline. The recovery preserved a 37-34 victory and set the Chargers on their way to a 6-0 start. In the middle of it all was Junior. He stood out even in defeat, recording one sack and a career-high 19 tackles in San Diego's first loss, a 20-15 setback in the rematch against the Broncos.

Things were going well. Real well. Maybe too well.

In late November, Junior pinched a nerve in his neck in a 23-17 loss to the New England Patriots. The injury was serious. Certain hits would send currents of pain streaming through his body and leave his left arm numb. At times, it appeared to be hanging limp from his shoulder.

It was so bad that in a December game against San Francisco, 49ers offensive tackle Harris Barton couldn't help but empathize with Junior. He looked at the proud linebacker in obvious pain and advised him not to risk further injury. The Chargers were headed for the playoffs, and Barton told Junior to save himself now so he could be ready later.

"I heard Harris but I didn't say anything to him," said Junior. "Pain is just part of football. If you can't deal with pain, then you can't play football."

Not all players were as caring as Barton. There were some who tried to take advantage of Junior. They talked down to him. They doubted him. They tried to exploit his injury.

To Junior, playing football is a matter of honor. So he was not going to leave the field unless he absolutely had to. If he had two good legs and one good arm, then there was no reason to stand on the sideline. You play on and do the best you can. You take names and numbers and remember that there will be a tomorrow.

"To know every day, going to work, if someone hit that shoulder it could go numb and you would be worthless was an obstacle that I had to overcome mentally and physically," said Junior. "To know that there was a player that you were facing

When it comes to football, Junior is anything but average. (AP/Wide World Photos)

that you had beaten so many times, and come to find out now you're an average player—that is something I've always been afraid of, being average.

"There were plays I could see happening before they happened and there was nothing I could do about it. People were talking about me, knowing that I'm hurt and knowing that I'm not all there, and it was tough. You picture them talking about you while you're down and mentally jot down names for the next time we come back around. I definitely did that. I'm not naming names, but there was a time where they took advantage of it. I still remember them today."

There was no way Seau was going to take himself off the field, not with the Chargers marching through the playoffs and headed to Pittsburgh for the AFC Championship Game.

Junior keeps an eye on the action. (Joe Robbins)

Super Bowl Bound

The Chargers were getting no respect as the AFC Championship Game approached. They beat the Pittsburgh Steelers in the regular-season finale, but now the Steelers were heavy favorites.

Steelers players called the loss in the season finale a fluke. They claimed that their coach, Bill Cowher, used a bunch of second- and third-string players because the team had already clinched a play-off berth.

Junior sacks John Elway. (AP/Wide World Photos)

The Steelers were so confident they boasted in radio, TV and newspaper interviews that they would win. Defensive end Ray Seals even boasted that San Diego would not score. Several of the players even recorded a Super Bowl rap video.

None of this sat well with the Chargers. Coach Bobby Ross even called a team meeting to discuss it. He told his players this was a defining moment. He spoke to their manhood and sense of pride. He urged his players to prove the critics wrong.

In the locker room before the game, Junior was silent. His neck and shoulder were bothering him, but he knew the Chargers might not ever get back to this point, and he was not about to squander the opportunity.

On the first play after the kickoff, Junior broke through the line of scrimmage and threw running back Barry Foster for a loss. It was the first of many big plays he would make. He finished with 16 tackles, 12 of them unassisted, as the Chargers silenced the critics with a 17-13 victory to advance to the Super Bowl for the first time in the franchise's history.

The Chargers would lose to the 49ers two weeks later in Miami, but the memory of Pittsburgh would never be forgotten. Junior was numb after that game, and not because of his arm. Every player dreams of reaching a Super Bowl, and now Junior was going. He could have floated back to San Diego on a cloud.

As the team plane neared San Diego, the players looked out the windows to see the dark night broken by a trail of headlights leading to San Diego Jack Murphy Stadium, where an overflow crowd of 61,000 was waiting to thank the players and coaches.

"You would have thought it was New York or something, and it was our hometown," said Junior. "To go to the stadium and then finally get into the stadium, I get chills every time I think about it. It's something that will never be repeated. We can go back to the Super Bowl and we can have the same response from the public, but we won't feel that same thing, because the first time is special. I got up there on the mike, I said what I had to say and then I looked around and there was San Diego.

"When we were leaving the stadium, the people that couldn't get in the stadium were lined up along the roads. It was a feeling that I'm going to cherish forever. If there's one memorable moment that I'm going to cherish throughout my career, that was it. Everyone fighting for one goal and achieving it. Everyone feeling it, the success, just the admiration for each other, of not taking anything for themselves, but sharing it with everybody.

"It's easy to go out there and take your gift or talent and achieve a goal. But when you're able to take a group and be able to achieve it, that's something you cannot explain. That's a champion to me. All the individual accolades I receive are fine and dandy. But until we get somewhere where we can where a ring and win, that's the feeling you want. That is my drug of life. Winning."

After the win in Pittsburgh, Junior couldn't wait to see his father. The picture of him walking into San Diego Jack Murphy Stadium with the crowd cheering and his arms around his mother and father remains one of his favorites.

Normally after a victory, Tiaina shakes hands with his son and congratulates him. He did neither this time. No handshake. No words.

"He's so consistent," said Junior. "He's not up and down. That guy is stone cold, you know, no feeling, you know, good job. Rarely smiles. But I knew my dad was happy when he came up to me and he didn't handshake me. He gave me a hug. That's different for Dad. Dad doesn't like to show emotions. We can say 'I love you', and he says, OK. He's one of those types of Dad. But that's something I'm going to remember forever. It was just the hug. He finally gave me a hug."

All the adversity he had gone through suddenly seemed so far away. And whenever times get tough, Junior remembers the words of his father.

"My dad always says, 'You're going fail more than you succeed, son. So, if you don't have any humor in your life, it's going to be a long day,' said Junior. "Patience is a word that I'll never get used to, but when I'm forced to use it, I'm one of the

Junior enjoys the atmosphere while on the field at Stadium Australia, the official stadium for the 2000 Olympic Games in Sydney. (AP/Wide World Photos)

best at it."

Last year was one of those times. Not surprisingly, Junior came out on top.

Junior Seau Quick Facts

Name: Tiaina Seau, Jr.

Team: San Diego Chargers

Position: Linebacker

Number: 55

Height/Weight: 6' 3"/255 lbs.

Birthdate: January 19, 1969

Hometown: San Diego, California

Years in the League: 9

Drafted: First Round (5th overall)

College: University of Southern California

1998 Highlight: Named to eighth consecutive Pro Bowl. Made 115 tackles and one sack.

Statistical Highlight: Made 11 tackles and one sack against San Francisco in Super Bowl XXIX.

Little known for: Seau did not speak English until the age of seven, his family moved to American Samoa when Junior was young.

Junior Seau Career Statistics

Year	Team	G	Tack.-Asst.	Total	Sacks-Yds.	Int.-Yds.
1990	SD	16	61-24	85	1-12	0-0
1991	SD	16	111-18	129	7-42	0-0
1992	SD	15	79-23	102	4.5-22	2-51
1993	SD	16	108-21	129	0-0	2-58
1994	SD	16	124-31	155	5.5-27.5	0-0
1995	SD	16	111-18	129	2-10	2-5
1996	SD	15	110-28	138	7-41	2-18
1997	SD	15	84-13	97	7-40	2-33
1998	SD	16	92-23	115	3.5-29	0-0
TOTAL		**141**	**880-199**	**1,079**	**37.5-223.5**	**10-165**

Junior Seau's NFL Statistics

1998

Date	Opp	TK	A	Sack	SackYd	Int
09/06/98	Buf	2	2	0.0	0.0	0
09/13/98	@Ten	4	1	0.0	0.0	0
09/20/98	@KC	8	0	0.0	0.0	0
09/27/98	NYN	12	0	0.0	0.0	0
10/04/98	@Ind	5	2	0.0	0.0	0
10/11/98	@Oak	6	1	0.0	0.0	0
10/18/98	Phi	6	4	0.5	4.0	0
10/25/98	Sea	7	0	0.0	0.0	0
11/08/98	@Den	5	2	1.0	9.0	0
11/15/98	Bal	4	1	0.0	0.0	0
11/22/98	KC	7	1	0.0	0.0	0
11/29/98	Den	4	0	1.0	13.0	0
12/06/98	@Was	5	0	1.0	3.0	0
12/13/98	@Sea	7	1	0.0	0.0	0
12/20/98	Oak	4	4	0.0	0.0	0
12/27/98	@Ari	6	4	0.0	0.0	0
TOTAL		16	92	23	3.5	29.0	0

1997

Date	Opp	TK	A	Sack	SackYd	Int
09/07/97	@NO	9	2	1.0	5.0	0
09/14/97	Car	6	0	0.0	0.0	1
09/21/97	@Sea	2	1	1.0	2.0	0
09/28/97	Bal	4	0	1.0	7.0	0
10/05/97	@Oak	8	1	1.0	8.0	0
10/16/97	@KC	4	0	0.0	0.0	0
10/26/97	Ind	6	0	0.0	0.0	0
11/02/97	@Cin	6	1	1.0	0.0	0
11/09/97	Sea	6	1	1.0	7.0	0
11/16/97	Oak	9	1	0.0	0.0	0
11/23/97	@SF	11	2	1.0	9.0	0
11/30/97	Den	4	1	0.0	0.0	0
12/07/97	Atl	5	0	0.0	0.0	0
12/14/97	KC	2	2	0.0	0.0	0
12/21/97	@Den	2	1	0.0	0.0	1
TOTAL	15	110	28	7.0	41.0	2

1996

Date	Opp	TK	A	Sack	SackYd	Int
09/01/96	Sea	2	1	1.0	0.0	0
09/08/96	Cin	4	1	0.0	0.0	0
09/15/96	@GB	10	2	0.0	0.0	0
09/22/96	@Oak	8	1	1.0	8.0	0
09/29/96	KC	9	3	1.0	6.0	2
10/06/96	@Den	8	0	0.0	0.0	0
10/21/96	Oak	9	2	0.0	0.0	0
11/03/96	@Ind	5	0	2.0	13.0	0
11/11/96	Det	1	0	0.0	0.0	0
11/17/96	TB	9	6	0.0	0.0	0
11/24/96	@KC	5	2	0.0	0.0	0
12/01/96	NE	14	0	0.0	0.0	0
12/08/96	@Pit	10	4	0.0	0.0	0
12/14/96	@Chi	11	3	2.0	14.0	0
12/22/96	Den	5	3	0.0	0.0	0

TOTAL	G	TK	A	Sack	SackYd	Int
	15	110	28	7.0	41.0	2

Baseball Superstar Series Titles

Collect Them All!

___ Mark McGwire: Mac Attack!

___ #1 *Derek Jeter: The Yankee Kid*

___ #2 *Ken Griffey Jr.: The Home Run Kid*

___ #3 *Randy Johnson: Arizona Heat!*

___ #4 *Sammy Sosa: Slammin' Sammy*

___ #5 *Bernie Williams: Quiet Superstar*

___ #6 *Omar Vizquel: The Man with the Golden Glove*

___ #7 *Mo Vaughn: Angel on a Mission*

___ #8 *Pedro Martinez: Throwing Strikes*

___ #9 *Juan Gonzalez: Juan Gone!*

___ #10 *Tony Gwynn: Mr. Padre*

___ #11 *Kevin Brown: Kevin with a "K"*

___ #12 *Mike Piazza: Mike and the Mets*

___ #13 *Larry Walker: Canadian Rocky*

___ #14 *Nomar Garciaparra: High 5!*

___ #15 *Sandy and Roberto Alomar: Baseball Brothers*

___ #16 *Mark Grace: Winning with Grace*

___ #17 *Curt Schilling: Phillie Phire!*

___ #18 *Alex Rodriguez: A+ Shortstop*

___ #19 *Roger Clemens: Rocket!*

Only $4.95 per book!

Football Superstar Series Titles
Collect Them All!

____ #1 *Ed McCaffrey: Catching a Star*

____ #3 *Peyton Manning: Passing Legacy*

____ #4 *Jake Plummer: Comeback Cardinal*

____ #5 *Mark Brunell: Super Southpaw*

____ #6 *Drew Bledsoe: Patriot Rifle*

____ #7 *Junior Seau: Overcoming the Odds*

____ #8 *Marshall Faulk: Rushing to Glory*

Only $4.95 per book!

Call Toll Free: 1-877-424-BOOK (2665) or visit us at www.sportspublishinginc.com